In the great orchestra we call life,
you have an instrument and a song,
and you owe it to God to
play them both sublimely.

MAX LUCADO

choices

The LORD says, "I will guide you along the best pathway for your life. I will advise you and watch over you."

PSALM 32:8 NLT

Presented to

Presented by

Date

Think positively and masterfully,
with confidence and faith, and life becomes
more secure, more fraught with action,
richer in achievement and experience.

EDDIE RICKENBACKER

Success
is not built on what we
accomplish for ourselves.
Its foundation lies in what
we do for others.

DANNY THOMAS

Don't lose sight of good planning and insight.
Hang on to them, for they fill you with life
and bring you honor and respect.

PROVERBS 3:21–22 NLT

opportunity

You shall walk in all the ways which the LORD your God has commanded you, that you may live and that it may be well with you, and that you may prolong your days in the land which you shall possess.

DEUTERONOMY 5:33 NKJV

Each of us makes a *difference.*
It is from numberless acts of courage and
belief that human history is shaped.

ROBERT F. KENNEDY

If any of you need wisdom, you should *ask God,*
and it will be given to you. God is generous
and won't correct you for asking.

JAMES 1:5 CEV

courage

I command you—be *strong* and *courageous!*

Do not be afraid or discouraged.

For the LORD your God is with you wherever you go.

JOSHUA 1:9 NLT

The real *secret* of success is enthusiasm. Yes, more than enthusiasm, I would say excitement. I like to see people get excited. When they get excited they make a success of their lives.

WALTER CHRYSLER

enthusiasm

One day at a time,
begun on bended knee,
touching the throne of God,
in praise and with plea.

One day at a time,

with good thoughts to guide,

and a heart filled with love,

going forth side by side.

One day at a time,

my life in God's hand,

knowing his purpose,

following his plan.

God can make you *anything* you want to be,
but you have to put everything in God's hands.

MAHALIA JACKSON

Put on the new self, which in the likeness of God has
been created in righteousness and holiness of the truth.

EPHESIANS 4:24 NASB

I hope in You, O LORD;
You will answer,
O Lord my God.

PSALM 38:15 NASB

A diploma is not a certificate of right to special favor and profit in the world, but rather a commission to service.

WARREN G. HARDING

Stand at the crossroads and look. Ask for the ancient paths and where the best road is. Walk in it, and you will live in peace.

JEREMIAH 6:16 GNT

Not by their own sword did they win the land, nor did their own arm give them victory; but your right hand, and your arm, and the light of your countenance, for you delighted in them.

PSALM 44:3 NRSV

Many persons have a wrong idea of what constitutes true *happiness*. It is not attained through self-gratification but through fidelity to a worthy purpose.

HELEN KELLER

purpose

I ask you to decide . . . whether you will be an anvil—
or a hammer. The question is whether you are to be a
hammer—whether you are to give to the world in
which you were reared and educated the broadest possible
benefits of that education.

JOHN F. KENNEDY

When you find me, you find life, real life, to say nothing of
GOD's good pleasure.

PROVERBS 8:35 THE MESSAGE

The best side of me is
the inside of me.

Inside of me, God resides
and love abides.
It is there faith is true
and life is new.

Inside of me, I am known
and the way is shown.
It is there I am led
and my soul is fed.

Inside of me, joy is near
and peace is dear.
It is there God lives,
and gives and gives.

The best side of me is
the *inside of me.*

You brought me more happiness

than a rich harvest of grain and grapes.

I can lie down and sleep soundly because you,

LORD, will keep me safe.

PSALM 4:7–8 CEV

I always tell my graduating young people,
"Walk proudly in the light."

MARY MCLEOD BETHUNE

The LORD is your keeper; the LORD is your shade at your right hand. The sun shall not strike you by day, nor the moon by night.

Unless each day can be looked back upon

by an individual as one in which he has had

some fun, some joy, some real satisfaction,

that day is a loss.

DWIGHT D. EISENHOWER

If God is for us, who can be against us? He who did not spare his own Son, but gave him up for us all—how will he not also, along with him, graciously give us all things?

ROMANS 8:31–32 NIV

satisfaction

You shall go out in joy, and be led back in peace; the mountains and the hills before you shall burst into song, and all the trees of the field shall clap their hands.

ISAIAH 55:12 NRSV

peace

My alphabet starts with this letter called yuzz. It's the letter I use to spell yuzz-a-ma-tuzz. You'll be sort of surprised what there is to be found once you go beyond "Z" and start poking around!

DR. SEUSS

I have missed over 9,000 shots, lost almost 300 games,
on 26 occasions have been entrusted to take the game winning
shot and missed. I have failed over and over again in my life.
And that is why I succeed.

MICHAEL JORDAN

A good name is to be chosen rather than great
riches, loving favor rather than silver and gold.

PROVERBS 22:1 NKJV

God's love enfolds me;
God's power upholds me.

God's wisdom guides my way;
God's light brightens my day.

God's peace quiets the storm;
God's care makes me warm.

God's strength helps me cope;
God's promise gives me hope.

God is great;
God is good.

greatness

A great deal of talent is lost to the world for want of a little courage.

SYDNEY SMITH

The LORD gives his people strength. The LORD blesses them with peace.

PSALM 29:11 NLT

Let the one the Lord loves *rest* safely in him.
The Lord *guards* him all day long.
The one the Lord loves rests in his arms.

DEUTERONOMY 33:12 NIrV

rest

The fireworks begin today. Each diploma
is a lighted match. Each one of you is a fuse.

ED KOCH

Do not be anxious about anything, but in everything, by prayer
and petition, with thanksgiving, present your requests to God.
And the peace of God, which transcends all understanding,
will guard your hearts and your minds in Christ Jesus.

PHILIPPIANS 4:6–7 NIV

Happy are those who live pure lives,

who follow the LORD's teachings.

Happy are those who keep his rules,

who try to obey him with their whole heart.

PSALM 119:1–2 NCV

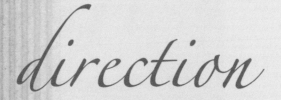
direction

The bee is more honored than other animals, not because she labors, but because she labors for others.

SAINT JOHN CHRYSOSTOM

Pour out your heart to God and tell Him how you *feel.* Be real, be honest, and when you get it all out, you'll start to feel the gradual covering of God's comforting presence.

BILL HYBELS

I am with you and will keep you wherever you go, and will bring you back to this land; for I will not leave you until I have done what I have promised you.

GENESIS 28:15 NASB

be real

God is good and kind.
In his embrace I find
more love than I thought,
strength to do what I ought.

God is love and heart,
is with me from the start.
In God I trust and believe;
from God I expect and receive.

God is sure and true,
and will guide me through
to where I need to be,
to what I need to see.

Congratulations Graduate You Did It!
ISBN 1-40372-019-3

Published in 2006 by Spirit Press, an imprint of Dalmatian Press, LLC.
Copyright © 2006 Dalmatian Press, LLC. Franklin, Tennessee 37067.

Editor: Lila Empson
Compiler: Phillip H. Barnhart
Design: Diane Whisner, Tulsa, Oklahoma

Printed in China

06 07 08 09 LPU 10 9 8 7 6 5 4 3 2 1

14942